BRITISH
MOTORING

THE GOLDEN AGE

Brian Staples, current owner of this 1922 11.4 Humber, kindly allows the author and his wife to renew their ties with 'Little Mo' at a Humber Register meet in 2001. *(The Humber Register)*

BRITISH MOTORING

THE GOLDEN AGE

A.B. DEMAUS

The
History
Press

First published 2010

The History Press
The Mill, Brimscombe Port
Stroud, Gloucestershire, GL5 2QG
www.thehistorypress.co.uk

British Library Cataloguing in Publication Data.
A catalogue record for this book is available from the British Library.

isbn 978 0 7524 5133 6

Typesetting and origination by The History Press
Printed in Great Britain
Manufacturing managed by Jellyfish Print Solutions Ltd

Contents

Acknowledgments

The author's archive of motoring photographs has been built up over many years and kind friends and fellow enthusiasts have generously contributed to the collection. Individual photographs are each acknowledged separately. Where no such acknowledgement appears, the photograph had no attribution when found or purchased and has defied further research. Inevitably there will be some errors or omissions for which sincere apologies are offered.

This Malvernia car, the origins of which pre-date the 1890s, was built by T.C. Santler in Malvern. Miraculously it still survives. *(F.W. Ring-Santler)*

Introduction

It is a fortunate fact of history that the art of the photographer, both professional and amateur, had reached proficiency by the time the motor car became a practicality in the last decade of the nineteenth century. It is thanks to innumerable such photographers that the illustrations in this book are possible as a record of forty years of social change that the motor car has accelerated and, indeed, played a vital role in. Whereas professional photographs are invariably of excellent quality, amateur pictures are of variable standard, but are often a more intimate and personal link between the car and its owner's family and their activities.

Photographs open your eyes and minds to history.

1

Early Days

Karl Benz is credited with being the first to design a sound and practical internal combustion engine. This early model ably illustrates why early cars were often referred to as 'horseless carriages'.

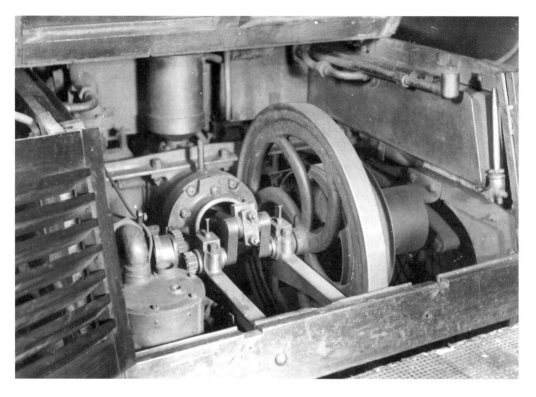

Here the mysteries of its engine are laid bare.

An unidentified tiller-steered car of about 1898. This form of seating layout was termed 'vis-à-vis'. The presence of the watering can suggests water cooling for the engine. *(Mrs G. Moore)*

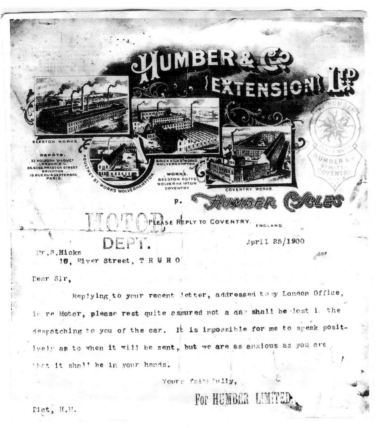

A letter dated 25 April 1900 from Humber (Extension) Ltd to a prospective customer in Truro. Humber, despite having dallied with petrol engines from 1896, approached the twentieth century in troubled mood, with a disastrous factory fire, a desperate need to rationalise production and with boardroom problems. *(The Humber Register)*

Humber's first car, 1900. *(D. Hales)*

Could this be the Chevalier René de Knyff peering at this early Panhard et Levassor at an unidentified location?

Early veteran car cockpits were uncomplicated, though in many cases the controls would be unfamiliar to the motorist of today. The cockpit of this 1903 Humberette is uncluttered and has no instrumentation whatsoever.

This engine-less, solid-tyred, chain-driven veteran car at an unknown location, alas, remains unidentified.

A White steam car with a full complement of passengers is about to set off from Moraston House, Ross-on-Wye, on a fine summer's day. Note the complete lack of weather protection.

Seen here is an early Panhard et Levassor in a country setting in Cornwall.

Perhaps the Guinness brothers' long association with the racing Darracqs and others from the same stable stemmed from happy memories of this early family car, a 1903 16hp. *(The Guinness Archives)*

This Decauville was a widely travelled car but is seen here in the grounds of its Kidderminster owner's home. *(MAC)*

This Mercedes is set against the splendid scenery of Scotland while its owner admires the view. He was Frederick Rich from Cornwall. The car was registered AF78 and was painted white.

The car is a 20hp Bayard with a Talbot badge, of 1907–8, known as a Clement-Bayard. At the wheel is Barbara Lea Smith, later the 14th Lady Dudley. *(The Lord Dudley)*

This veteran Wolseley registered in East Suffolk (BJ) has brought the cottagers out to look, but they don't appear to be entirely strangers to the motorist. *(A. Townsend)*

A single-cylinder Rover of about 1905 bears a London registration, but poses here in a country lane.
The bodywork is a swing-seat tonneau and the handle at the back of the front seat, when unlocked,
allows the rear part of the body to swing in an arc to allow ingress and exit.

A rather formal domestic scene in Knighton-on-Teme, Worcestershire. The car partly visible is a
Minerva. *(MAC)*

This 1907 10/12hp Coventry Humber with its lady driver is appropriately registered as CJ 254, a Herefordshire registration, as it pauses outside a house in Ross-on-Wye. *(F. Druce)*

Parliamentary candidates soon began to see that the motor car had become reasonably reliable and its use made canvassing a great deal easier. Here a candidate in the 1906 election has attracted quite a crowd.

A meet of the Hawkstone Otter Hounds at Leintwardine on the River Teme in about 1912.
A ubiquitous Model-T Ford stands to the right. AW 124 is a Shropshire issue, here with a
wagonette body. To the left is a large Minerva landaulette which carries the Shropshire plate AW7.
(The Leintwardine History Soceity)

This 20hp Rover carries a Herefordshire mark of early 1907 (CJ 418). It is approaching Kington from the east of the town. *(Kington Museum)*

Here is a delightful study of a 1913 11hp Humber. Worthy of remark is the device on the windscreen which is directly in the line of vision of the driver. It is a rectangular 'clear vision' aperture for wet-weather use before the days of the windscreen wiper, a gadget that came into more common use after the First World War. *(The Humber Register)*

This very smartly turned out Progress Quadricycle was registered AF77 in Cornwall in 1904. It appears to be in brand-new condition.

This early MMC boasts an auxiliary step above the main running-board to facilitate entry into the 'side entrance' tonneau.

A smartly dressed young couple grace this Morgan of about 1912. In addition to the normal acetylene sidelight, the car has a large headlamp centrally on the scuttle. *(The National Library of Wales)*

This is an American car, the RMC Underslung, which seems to wear its chassis 'upside down', resulting in a lower appearance. The choice of a cattleyard as a backdrop may indicate that the owner is a farmer. The car carries an 'FF' mark (Merionethshire) . . . *(The National Library of Wales)*

. . . as does this very handsome 12/16 Sunbeam as FF 272. *(Bruce Dowell)*

This Edwardian Singer poses in a wintry landscape. Note the electric sidelamps but acetylene headlamps. It carries a London (LK) mark. *(Lynn Hughes)*

This young lady is at the wheel of a Stellite, made by Electric & Ordnance Accessories Ltd which was a subsidiary of Wolseley. It was built between 1913 and 1919 with a 4-cylinder engine and 3-speed gears. The lady named the car Stella and it cost £285 in 1919.

The dickey on this Clement-Talbot of about 1912 at least has the benefit of the ample folded hood of the front compartment and is nicely finished and lined to match the rest of the car. It was photographed on 17 July 1913 on Teignmouth Parade.

2

Chauffeurs

DEAR OLD LADY (*having a lift—her first motor ride—as chauffeur signals a turn*). "Look here, young man—you keep both hands on the wheel. I'll tell you when it begins to rain."

(*The proprietors of Punch*)

An Edwardian chauffeur in uniform typical of the time. The full-length double-breasted greatcoat was essential weather protection. *(R. Smith)*

The 6-cylinder Coventry Humber of 1908 was a comparatively rare model. The chauffeur looks very proud of his car in a sparkling new condition, as well he might. *(The Humber Register)*

The chauffeur stands beside this early Panhard et Levassor with its crew of smartly dressed ladies, one of whom poses behind the wheel. 'K' is a Liverpool registration. *(F. Williams)*

This 1911 12/20 Humber is a landaulette with the division and all windows and the hood down. As this is an official Humber photograph it was probably taken in the works with the background erased. *(The Humber Register)*

This 1911 12/20 Humber is plying for hire as a taxi in Buenos Aires. Note the smartly dressed uniformed driver and the prominent taxi-meter on the screen pillar. Humbers enjoyed a flourishing export trade in the Edwardian years. *(The Humber Register)*

Opposite: A Wolseley-Siddeley, with a London mark (LB), in Hereford. The young lady behind the wheel will doubtless move to allow the chauffeur to take up her place. *(Bustin/Hereford)*

LB-8612

This picture by the well-known Hereford photographer Bustin was taken in the Palace Yard, one of his favourite locations. It portrays a rather angular Peugeot landaulette with division folded down, as are all windows and the hood. *(Bustin/Hereford)*

CHAUFFEUR. "I regret the car will not be available this afternoon, my lady."

MISTRESS. "Why? What's the matter?"

CHAUFFEUR. "Yesterday was one of his Lordship's days with the carburettor, my lady."

The chauffeur occupies the back seat in this picture of a 20hp Rolls-Royce tourer taken on Ranmore Common on 27 July 1928. *(C. Cottrell)*

Here is a very smart chauffeur at the wheel of an equally smart Crossley tourer, in about 1925.

This benign-looking chauffeur lovingly polishes the radiator of a 1928 14/40 Humber saloon. Of course, he wears gloves (for cleaning, not driving) while doing so. *(The Humber Register)*

3

Picnics & Pubs

The George Hotel, Birdlip, is the scene for a motor outing for delicate and crippled children of Cheltenham, given by the Bristol & Gloucester Automobile Club on 4 June 1910. *(Donald Bott Photography)*

A halt for refreshment for a Decauville on a day tour in the Welsh borders. *(MAC)*

All the ingredients for the picnic of the time are contained in this shot of a family with their 1910 12hp Humber – a pleasant spot in the country, sun and shade and what would seem to be an ample repast. The car was registered AB 1542 on 17 June 1910 and was finished in Humber green. *(The Humber Register)*

A 1909 12hp Humber registered in Worcestershire as AB 1151 and a Rex motorcycle with an 'FK' (Worcester city) mark, halt for a very spartan-looking picnic in wooded country. *(The Humber Register)*

A Humberette with its Worcester owner at the Talbot Hotel, Knighton-on-Teme, on what seems to be a rather bleak day. *(W.J. Bladder)*

A 1914 Humber 10hp and family take a roadside picnic in the Forest of Dean in that year. *(W.J. Bladder)*

The famous Fish Inn, atop Broadway Hill, is a halting place for a 1914 Humberette.

A well-stocked picnic for this family with their 10hp Humber in that fateful summer of 1914. (*W.J. Bladder*)

'Parties catered for' quotes the Red Lion Inn. Here they have a large party of Bayliss-Thomas owners, their cars stretching as far as the eye can see.

An Armstrong-Siddeley tourer rests outside the White Horse Hotel in Haslemere High Street.

It is difficult to be sure whether this picnic is just about to begin or just about to end. Either way, the lady in the front seat of this Fiat Tipo 501 tourer doesn't mean to leave the car.

A Jowett saloon, a 14/60 Lagonda and a Bullnose Morris gather outside the Avon Hotel in an unidentified town. *(VSCC)*

A Morris Six saloon tows the caravan while the owner of the Clyno saloon alongside prefers a tent in this pleasant rural scene of about 1930.

An Austin Twelve saloon with a London registration (GX) and towing a caravan has halted on the wide verge of the road. It seems that a picnic is about to start. *(Bird)*

A Lagonda LG45 saloon-de-ville forms the backdrop of this happy-looking family picnic on the Preseli Hills. The corgi looks pleased to return to its roots.

4

A Ride in the Dickey

The 6-cylinder ohc 24/90 Straker-Squire was a fine design beautifully built. This, a later example with fwb, has a capacious dickey seat. The car was owned at the time by a Mr G.F. Lomas of Ludlow, Shropshire. *(G.F. Lomas)*

This Edwardian Swift of about 1910 has a dickey seat which looks like something of an afterthought as it has not been painted to match the rest of the car. As the front compartment has no hood, the dickey would have been very exposed to the elements. *(Miss Wilkinson)*

The dickey seat passenger in this Métallurgique of a year or two later is accommodated within the bodywork. Note the rather crude step that gives access to the dickey. *(Lynn Hughes)*

This late Edwardian Calcott also gives the dickey seat passenger a very exposed ride.

A happy load in a Belsize two-seater and dickey in 1927.

This magnificent picture shows a coupé body on an 11.9hp Herbert chassis. These cars were made in 1916–17 by The Herbert Light Car Co. in north-west London. A handsome car but the dickey, when in use, was very exposed. *(B.K. Goodman)*

The position of the dickey so far aft and thus exposed is dictated by the car being a three-wheeler; uncomfortable nevertheless. *(H. Goodwin)*

An SV Humber 11.4 displays its very comfortably upholstered (in buttoned leather) dickey which even boasts arm rests. Humber's bodywork was always superb. *(The Humber Register)*

This early 1920s two-seater and dickey takes two middle-aged ladies in apparent comfort. Unusually, the car has torpedo sidelights on the wings and a pair of egg-shaped ones on the scuttle.

This GN accommodates two in the front with a third person and a large dog in the dickey in a picture of 1922 at Crookham. *(J. Dearling)*

This very well-laden AC, in which the dickey is crammed with luggage, has just climbed 'Rest and be Thankful', the notorious Scottish hill, in 1925. *(C. Cottrell)*

This all-male party, with a Bayliss-Thomas 2/3-seater of the early 1920s, seem to be enjoying a rather alcoholic picnic. One wonders what else lurks in the dickey.

The 11/22 Wolseley of the early 1920s has a properly upholstered dickey in which, if the hood is down, as here, the occupant is fully exposed to the slipstream.

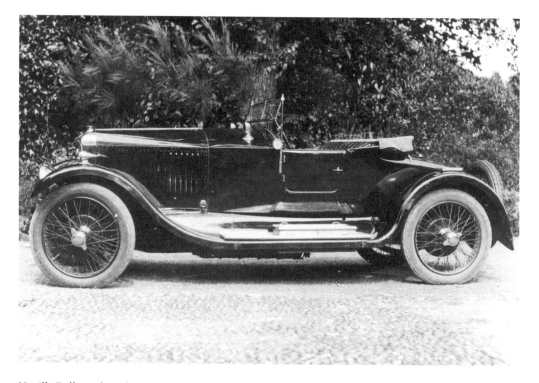

Neville Rollason's 30/98 Vauxhall two-seater, registration number NX 5080. *(G.S. Boston)*

5

Pride of Ownership

Pride of ownership was by no means confined to owners of large and expensive cars. Who could look more delighted than this young lady with her Cup Model Austin Seven?

Two schoolboys discuss the merits of this very smart 14/40 Lea-Francis tourer, or perhaps one is saying 'My dad's car is a lot faster!' *(Mrs G. Moore)*

The owner of this Vauxhall expresses his pride by body language. He might be Mr Toad himself!

The polished aluminium wheel discs enhance the appearance of this fabric-bodied (Gordon England) 3-litre Bentley saloon in a pleasingly unfussy style. *(E. Widgery)*

Here is a very handsome and compact 1½-litre Invicta that seems to be in brand-new order. The body has four doors and is neatly finished off with a tonneau cover and a hoodbag. *(R.H. Van den Akker)*

Gordon England built this handsome sports body on a 3-litre Invicta for Prince Cantacuzino. Individual step-boards for each door have taken the place of running-boards and make for a much neater appearance. *(E. Widgery)*

The owner of this 1930 Humber Snipe 4-door Weymann coupé shows his appreciation by fitting numerous extras – the radiator stoneguard, two extra horns and a fire extinguisher on the nearside running-board.

The owner of this Talbot sports saloon has similarly shown his pride and joy in the car by the fitting of extra lamps and a running-board-mounted Pyrene fire extinguisher.

A massive Minerva with a London (UV) mark, seen with owner Michael Haworth-Booth on a Continental tour, couldn't fail to impress. (M. Haworth-Booth)

To own a very handsome fixed-head coupé Rolls-Royce Silver Ghost with a resplendent 'flying lady' mascot cannot fail to delight.

6

Motorcycles

Here a rider with a Vindec Special registered P 819 (Surrey) surmounts Blockley Hill near Broadway, which seems to have defeated two early cars.

This very rare machine is a Wilkinson TAC 4-cylinder motorcycle made by the famous sword makers. This one dates from 1920 and carries a London mark.

This Herefordshire-registered Motosacoche carries a young man (who appears to have left his alternative headgear on the ground) with his young lady riding sidesaddle on the pillion, as was normal then.

Two lady competitors thread the streets of Taunton in the 1912 six-days trial. *(A.R. Abbott)*

A.C. Wright of Kidderminster was a very active competition rider who is portrayed with G. Nickson with his Wright-Blumfield bike, AB 1120.

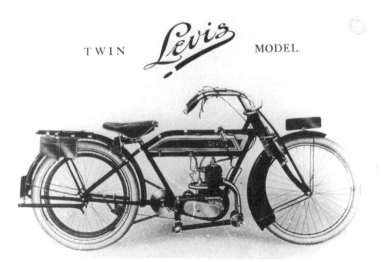

TWIN *Levis* MODEL.

The Levis was a very popular lightweight machine made from 1913 to the mid-1920s. This is a trade card for the firm. *(R. Howard)*

Here A.B. Sayce rides his Worcestershire-registered (AB 2385) Rudge-Multi with his wife in the wicker sidecar. The air-cooled Humberette on trade plates (FK-C1) belongs to his wife's family. *(Worcester RO)*

F.W. Giles brings his 3½hp Triumph up Hopton Bank, near Cleobury Mortimer, Shropshire.

A Worcestershire-registered Bradbury is the focus for two young motorcyclists, both with caps flat-a-back and cigarettes. They have met a third party apparently in the middle of nowhere! The bike dates from mid-1912.

Members of the Redditch & DMCC, mostly with BSA and Royal Enfield machines, descend into the Teme Valley at Stockton-on-Teme, 1913. *(E.W. Viles)*

This Berkshire-registered (BL) bike of about 1910 is very smartly turned out, its young rider even more so, but it is unlikely that he actually rode it in this garb.

This AJS was registered as FO 2336 (Radnorshire) on 7 February 1929. Here it is seen in Aymestrey, Herefordshire, when almost new. *(Leintwardine Local History Society)*

A middle-aged gentleman and his wife take to the country with this big AJS V-twin, with a Worcester city mark of FK 1067. *(G.D. Smith)*

A variation on the same theme, this time a big-twin P & M with sidecar, registered in Huddersfield.

Charlie Sgonina competes with his 3½hp Triumph in the 1921 Manx TT. *(Mrs C. Sgonina)*

Charlie Sgonina, Welsh ace motorcyclist, astride an early version of his SS (Sgonina Special), which he was later to develop into a very potent machine indeed. Luckily it still survives. *(Mrs C. Sgonina)*

Rosedale Abbey Bank, Yorkshire, was a very steep track with an appallingly bad surface, clearly visible in this shot.

Two Abingdon King Dick riders join a gathering of cars at a northern location. A tall Austin landaulette is visible on the left with a two-seater Newey on the right. *(Mrs G. Moore)*

George Dance, one of Sunbeam's works riders, established a formidable reputation for his successes in speed events and trials, where he gained innumerable trophies for best performance of the day. He is seen here, in white sweater, beside his early OHV Sprint Sunbeam at a Welsh event with, as usual, admirers around him. *(The Dance Archives)*

The inimitable George Dance with a Sunbeam on test at Enville Common, Staffordshire, in about 1929. *(Mrs J. Romsey)*

Obviously this young man is a sporting enthusiast with his fine Sunbeam, leather coat, goggles, muffler and leggings. *(R. Chapman)*

A halt by the wayside for this rider who is cheerfully adding some more air to the back tyre.

The 2-cylinder, 2-stroke, 2-speed Scott was a distinctive quality machine that earned a devoted following. Cooling was by water and the radiator was below the steering head in order to catch the benefits of the slipstream. *(G.S. Boston)*

Here Bert Denley, a well-known and accomplished racing man, is seen at Brooklands with his Norton and sidecar. *(W. Gibbs)*

This very purposeful-looking bike is the NUT (Newcastle-upon-Tyne) registered X 1914 with which Hugh Mason won the 1913 Junior TT. It has been updated for use by a Worcestershire motorcyclist in the early 1920s.

Some competitive motorcyclists favoured white sweaters, as does this rider of a Triumph at an unknown rural location. *(P. Bartlett)*

This BSA outfit, registered CJ8093 in Herefordshire, is seen here with its original owner in Ledbury. He continued to use it until he was of quite an advanced age.

7

Garage & Workshop

A rare Villiers-engined Cotton motorcycle stands
outside this well-stocked garage in Bromyard,
1922.

A Herefordshire trade plate 067 CJ adorns this Bullnose Morris in Edmund Williams' Bromyard garage. An early Austin Seven can be seen in the showroom window.

An unidentified but attractively-bodied sports two-seater stands outside premises that appear to be more those of a cycle agent rather than a garage.

As this advertising card proclaims, many who started in the motorcycle business progressed to the motor trade.

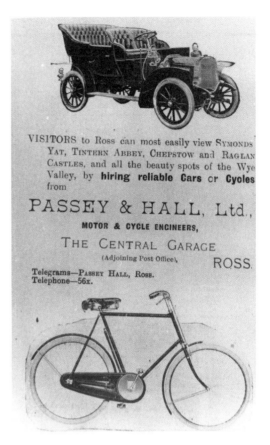

A.W. Marriott's garage in Hereford, in about 1904. The wooden crates contain 2-gallon petrol cans (Carburine Motor Spirit?) delivered by rail. The railway companies would only deliver on one or two (varied) days of the week. Note the CTC plaque on the wall.
(A.W. Marriott)

An early Belsize with a lofty landaulette body is seen in the premises of W.J. Bladder, Sidbury, Worcester. *(W.J. Bladder)*

The Central Garage, Llandeilo, receives a new batch of Willys-Overland cars. Oddly, some are on trade plates as might be expected but others carry Stockport (DB) numbers, where the British version was made after an alliance with Crossley. *(National Library of Wales)*

This very smart 1931 M-type MG Midget boasts a quick-action radiator filling cap with a coiled tube vent, a bonnet strap and neat tonneau cover. It carries a Shropshire (NT) trade plate. Strict conditions were laid down regarding the use of trade plates by bona fide garages and traders.

This Riley 'Redwing' two-seater has come to Watson's Motor Works in Leominster, Herefordshire, for repair . . . *(Watson's Motor Works)*

. . . which was duly carried out. The result: complete apart from the windscreen and a spare tyre at this stage. *(Watson's Motor Works)*

The motorcycle with a competition number and a crash-hatted rider suggest a strong motorcycle interest, but the words on the sliding door suggest a wider field of activity.

Motorcycles are prominent here too, but the interior reveals a late Clyno (right) beside an earlier Darracq with a Herefordshire (CJ) plate. *(F. Williams)*

A pity about the folds in this old photograph, but the premises and the fine Herefordshire (CJ) registered Daimler tourer are worthwhile. *(Ross Engineering Co. Ltd)*

This handsome H.E. is seen in June 1933 at a garage in Leominster, Herefordshire. *(M. Conod)*

A call for petrol. An Alvis 12/50 with a two-seater and dickey body calls in for fuel replenishment. The petrol tank was under the bonnet, feeding the carburettor by gravity – hence the open bonnet. Note the hand-operated petrol pumps.

8

Factory & Showroom

A Delaunay-Belleville stands in all its nakedness alongside a limousine on the firm's stand at the Salon de l'Automobile, 1904. They were always very impressive cars.

A scene photographed in the body shop of Humber Ltd, in 1909. A variety of partly assembled bodies may be seen. The workforce has assembled to face the camera to avoid the inevitable out-of-focus blurring that would have marred an 'action' photograph. *(The Humber Register)*

A scene in the works of a little-known make, the Phoenix, made in Letchworth, Hertfordshire. This is their brand-new 18hp tourer in front of a white screen for photographic purposes (1922) . . . *(R.C. Gray)*

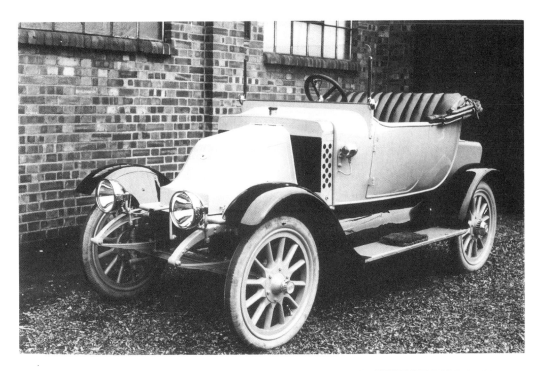

. . . while here is their smaller
11.9hp car, one of the few to
espouse the radiator-behind-engine
layout as late as 1921. *(R.C. Gray)*

Here one of Lionel Martin's delectable
Aston Martins stands in front of the
Bamford & Martin Works at
53 Abingdon Road, Kensington.
(Addis/Henley Coll)

Here, work is in progress on the racer 'Bunny' (with cowled radiator) and another, later, car may be glimpsed in the background. So much effort went into the firm's racing activities that production of cars for the public was slow to start.

Cyril Paul's sprint Beardmore displays its much drilled and lightened chassis in the Beardmore Works. The forward-sloping radiator filler was a Beardmore feature at the time. *(W. Gibbs)*

The impressive entrance hall at the Stoke Works of Humber Ltd, Coventry. On the left is a 9-cylinder Bentley aeroplane engine that Humber, among others, made during the First World War. Suspended overhead is an Avro 504, many of which were made by the firm. *(The Humber Register)*

A solitary lady works among the male draughtsmen in the Drawing Office, 1922. *(The Humber Register)*

Not surprisingly, the typists' department was exclusively staffed by women under Miss E. Redfern, the chief typist. *(The Humber Register)*

The trim shop in the Humber Works in about 1925. The standard of bodywork, both open and closed, was one of the make's most notable features. *(The Humber Register)*

In a momentary pause in activity, all eyes are turned towards the camera in the polishing shop, 1922. In the immediate foreground is a pile of polished hubcaps for the pre-war models. *(The Humber Register)*

Very strictly a male preserve, the wages counting house was situated at the rear of the main office block. Each employee was paid in one of the cylindrical cardboard containers seen in racks on the left. *(The Humber Register)*

The imposing frontage of Humber's showrooms at 52 Holborn Viaduct, London, 1922. Note the display of prices of cycles for that year. *(The Humber Register)*

A busy scene at Humber's major repair works at Kilburn. Examples of SV 15.9, 11.4 and 10hp cars
may be seen. All open cars, only one has the hood erected. The date is 1922. *(The Humber Register)*

9

Sport

Here we see C. Sangster with his 40hp Ariel tackle Shelsley
Walsh in Worcestershire. He took 137.8 seconds for his
climb on 13 July 1907. *(MAC)*

An evocative picture of a Coventry Humber taking a very active part in the Scottish Reliability Trials of 1909. *(R.F. Skelton)*

Kenelm Lee Guinness at the wheel of the Hillman-Coatalen that he drove in the 1908 'Four-Inch' TT race in the Isle of Man. *(S. Hall)*

Cecil Bianchi drove the sole Crossley representative in the 1914 TT race. Here, both rear wheels are airborne on Ballig Bridge on the first day of the race. *(Miss M. Burgess)*

The French GP was, of course, much more serious than the Tour de France, and here is Kenelm Lee Guinness with his mechanic, Cook, and their Sunbeam in 1913. *(The Guinness Archives)*

In the same year, Vauxhall, Sunbeam's great rivals, competed in the Coupé de l'Auto. Here Hancock, the firm's ace driver, waits for *le pesage*. His race number still has to be painted on.

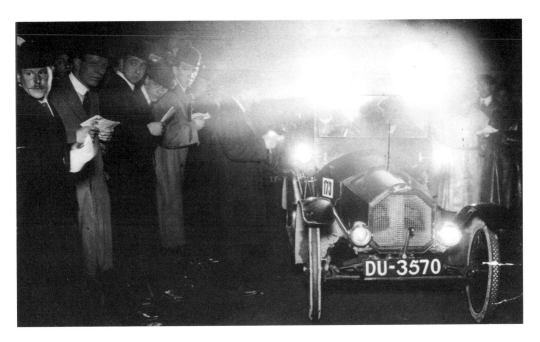

A night start for Sam Wright with his air-cooled Humberette with a Coventry (DU) plate in the London–Edinburgh Trial of 1913. *(A.R. Abbott)*

W.G. Tuck with one version of the several special Humbers used for Brooklands records, sometimes with an 11.9hp engine, sometimes with a 14hp for various classes. Tuck was Humber's most experienced driver. *(N.W. Portway)*

Here one of the Straker-Squires that had performed so well in the 1914 TT shows its pace at the very popular Caerphilly hillclimb. *(N.W. Portway)*

Here the entire workforce of Bamford & Martin, makers of Aston Martin cars, musters a little way
down the street. Jack Addis, the works foreman, is at the wheel of one of the 1922 French GP cars.
(Addis/Henley Coll)

Count 'Lou' Zborowski was well-known for his Brooklands appearances with his giant 'Chitty Chitty
Bang Bang', but here we see him with the very antithesis as he drives a slim and elegant Miller at
Monza in 1923. *(N.F. Murray)*

The driver of this sports Riley 'Redwing' finds time for a quiet snooze on the sands at Southport in 1925.

The scene on the wet sands at Pendine when Giulio Foresti (in beret by radiator) and helpers prepare his car 'Djelmo' for an attempt at the Land Speed Record in 1927. The car crashed and Foresti was lucky to survive. (*Lynn Hughes*)

George Duller in a 'Dutch Clog' Austin Seven at Brooklands in the 500 Miles race, 16 September 1933. *(A.B.I. Dick)*

From the tiny to the huge – Earl Howe's Mercedes-Benz at Shelsley Walsh in 1929. His times were 48.0s and 47.6s respectively. *(W. Gibbs)*

A Mathis tackles the formidable climb at Rosedale Abbey Bank in Yorkshire, in about 1922. *(Mrs G. Moore)*

The locations of some speed hillclimbs of the early 1920s were somewhat remote. Here is a Ford Model T fitted out as a mobile fish and chip van offering its wares to those attending Garrowby hillclimb on 23 June 1923. *(Mrs. G. Moore)*

'Chain-gang' Frazer-Nashes were frequent and successful performers in road trials. Here an example takes part in the 1934 Buxton trial. *(Mrs A.G. Gripper)*

The 1933 Light Car Race at Brooklands. Lined up for this we see, from left to right, an MG, a Vale Special and a Riley. The very low build of the Vale may be noted. At the wheel is Allan Gaspar, one of the founders of the company. *(David Cox)*

The racing Bentleys will always be associated with Le Mans, scene of so many of their triumphs. Here is no. 1 driven by Sir Henry 'Tim' Birkin and Woolf Barnato, seen refuelling their 6½ litre car. *(D.P. Brogden)*

Leo Villa, Malcolm Campbell's mechanic, poses beside the 12-cylinder 350hp record-breaking Sunbeam in this evocative shot taken at Pendine in July 1925. The very long-tailed body was built by Boulton & Paul and was tested in a wind tunnel. Campbell achieved a mean speed of 150.76mph over the flying mile, a world record at the time. *(Lynn Hughes)*

10

Social, Domestic & Pleasure

Weobley is one of Herefordshire's most attractive 'black and white' villages. A 1928 14/40 Humber tourer with a WK (Coventry) mark is surprisingly the only car in sight!

The photographer snapped! A Palladium 'Victory' model is the subject of a publicity shot outside
York Minster. *(Mrs G. Moore)*

A humble Morris Eight tourer snapped in a Worcester side-street. The absence of any kind of road
marking would be noteworthy today. The many flags perhaps indicate that it is 1937, the year of
George VI's coronation.

This Morris Eight Series E is portrayed approaching Fort Augustus when on an extended tour of Scotland in the fateful summer of 1939.

The Lanchester Straight 8 was a fine car, beautifully engineered as this nicely balanced example shows. *(S. Best)*

The owner of this Southampton-registered Essex saloon in very smart condition looks well pleased with it. The scenery looks similar to that of the New Forest.

A Morris Six saloon takes in the rugged mountain scenery of the Scottish Highlands in Glen Beag.

COUNTY OF WARWICK.

Licence No. **A/20558**   FEE **5/-**

DATE OF ISSUE

Licence to Drive a Motor Car or Cycle

MOTOR CAR ACT 1903, and ROADS ACT 1920.

Thomas Warwick CHENEY

of *"Kindeen" Tiddington Rd Stratford on Avon*

is hereby Licensed to drive a MOTOR CAR or CYCLE for the period of *Twelve Months*

from the .... day of 192 9

until the .... day of .... 193 .... *inclusive*

N.B.—The Licensee is responsible for the renewal of this Licence,
and no notice will be sent. It may be renewed any time
during the month preceding the date of expiration by
personal application or by forwarding Application Form,
Postal Order 5/-, and the old Licence, to Licences (Motors,
etc.) Office, 12, Northgate St., Warwick.
Office hours, 9—5. Saturdays, 9—12.

County Accountant.

This Licence should always be carried, as failure by the Driver of a Motor Car or Motor Cycle to produce a
Licence when demanded by a Police Constable renders him liable to a fine not exceeding £5. (Sec. 3(4) Motor
Car Act, 1903)

An essential requirement for any motorist is a driving licence. Mr Thomas Warwick Cheney was issued with this one on 28 August 1929. (*T.W. Cheney*)

French quality – a Delage tourer of about 1925. Note the three-panel screen, the double-twist horn, the toolbox projecting above and below the running-board and the two stepmats. The hood is neatly furled in a hood bag.

Saloon bodies on the early Bamford & Martin Astons were a rarity. Here the car's new owner poses proudly with the vehicle in a London street and also emphasises its low build. *(Addis/Henley Coll)*

An Austin Ten saloon is parked beside the Old Market Hall, Pembridge, Herefordshire, while an earlier car shelters beneath the hall's roof. Facing is the half-timbered New Inn. *(G. Dearling)*

This 30/98 Vauxhall, car OE99, registered NX 5080 (a Warwickshire registration), has its dickey crammed with luggage on a Continental holiday in the 1920s. *(G. Summers)*

Humber tourer KU2211, one of the last batch of fifty 15/40s built on the same chassis as the new 20/55. Thirty-three of them were tourers. The car wears the patina of several years' use, but is as it left the factory. Note the four-panel V-screen and the sidescreens which wound down into the doors. A bouquet of flowers graces the centre panel of the facia. *(L.P. Jarman)*

It is clearly winter but this 14/40 Vauxhall tourer remains open; the only concession to the season is the radiator muff, the usual method of retaining heat in the days before reliable chemical anti-freeze.

An Imperia saloon of about 1929 explores the peaceful waters of the River Thames at historic Runnymede. *(B.T. Batsford)*

Here is an SV Aston Martin, car no. 1959, registered in Cambridgeshire as ER 4506. *(N.F. Murray)*

When the Bertelli-designed cars came out, they set a fashion for cycle wings. Some owners, as in this case, updated earlier Bamford & Martin cars which did achieve some weight reduction.

The city of Worcester, looking towards Foregate Street, sometime between May 1928 and 1930 when the trams and tramlines disappeared. *(M. Dowty)*

Hereford High Town portrayed at about the same time. Note the Black & White coach which ran a daily service via Cheltenham to London.

This Morris Eight lived in Worcester and is seen here when it was about eighteen months old. The young lady driver captioned the photograph 'Afternoon trip to Wales'.

This early 1920s Rover tourer is still open with the hood neatly furled in its cover, despite the snow on the ground and on the bare branches. *(R. Judd)*

A 2-litre H.E. seen here when owned by Bryan Jeffrey, pictured in Cheshire. An unidentified sports car is in the background. *(G.S. Boston)*

The Model T Ford is older, but its passengers are of the 1920s, as testified not only by their garb but by the caption 'Bude, 1923'.

An early Bean two-seater with a 'GA' (Glasgow) mark emerges from its motor house, which looks as though it may have been part of a stableyard. The original photograph was captioned 'Eddy Burton at Buxton'. *(Ludlow Museum)*

This American Paige-Jewett saloon bears a 'DN' (York) registration and, apart from an additional pair of British sidelights on the wings, is typical of its breed.

Off the beaten track; seen here on a fine summer day in the country are a French-built Salmson and a Birmingham-registered Morris Cowley saloon of 1927.

This AC, seen about to depart on a journey, was nicknamed Alfred by its owner G. Taylor. The original photograph was by E.G. Box, June 1925. *(C. Cottrell)*

An elegant 3-litre, 2-ohc Sunbeam emerges from the motor house which bears the date of 1921. The owner of the car was Richard John Tinling Marston of the same family that made Sunbeams. *(Bruce Dowell)*

This very smart 'flatnose' Morris is at a small country gathering on what is obviously a very hot day. The screen is wide open as is the scuttle ventilator. It carries a Southampton mark (TR).

A Bayliss-Thomas tourer passes a new Birmingham trolleybus on the wet streets and tramlines.
Both vehicles carry Birmingham (OK) marks.

A motley bunch of youngsters gather on and around this heavily-built Peugeot saloon of the
late 1920s.

Renaults espoused the radiator-behind-engine layout longer than most. This is a fairly typical French small car of the period, seen in about 1926. (*G.H.J. Dearling*)

This AC two-seater of about 1925 has just posed at the summit of Beggar's Roost – a severe test of hillclimbing ability in the West Country. The driver seems suitably pleased.

An unusual but very attractive body is fitted to this 12/50 Alvis. The car was at one time owned by Norman 'Fluffy' Longfield, a stalwart of the Ilkley & District MCC. *(G.S. Boston)*

An Austin Seven chummy with a York (DN) mark and in very smart order takes two middle-aged occupants down some narrow lanes.

Two families link up here on a fine summer day in the late 1920s. The cars are a 6-cylinder Essex and a handsome Voisin saloon. *(Mrs G. Moore)*

Here we see a fine 3-litre Invicta with a substantial dhc body with the hood folded down. A bonnet strap on such a car was a little unusual.

These two sporting young ladies occupy a sports model Autocrat. It is winter time but they are both well wrapped up. *(A.J.A. Pearson)*

The two masked headlamps of this 3-litre Bentley tell us that war is again upon us. The car's owner, seen here, was a doctor, so had essential petrol. The cat on the bonnet adds a humorous touch. *(Lynn Hughes)*

11

An Irish Envoi

W.J. Bladder had a cycle and motor business in Worcester. J. Mecredy invited him to see the 1903
Gordon Bennett race in Ireland. Here is the Holyhead–Dublin steamer that brought him.
(W.J. Bladder)

This Mercedes in which the German driver Jenatzy won the 1903 Gordon Bennett race in Ireland, has nothing to shelter its occupants, although the riding mechanic in his outrigged seat occupies a lower position than the driver. This was in the interests of lowering the wind resistance rather than a concession to comfort. The nearside front wheel is equipped with a metal mudguard and leather shields to deflect flying stones. It is photographed in Ireland after the race.

The first road race of international importance to be held in the British Isles was the Gordon Bennett race of 1903, covering 327.5 miles on a course centred on the Irish town of Athy, County Kildare. Restrictive legislation on the mainland dictated this choice. Here we see the Mors driven by Gabriel at The Moat of Ardscull, Athy. The race was won by Jenatzy in a Mercedes at an overall average speed of 49.2mph. Gabriel was fourth at 45.3mph.

Here is Jenatzy, the ultimate winner, with his Mercedes at The Moat of Ardscull on the course. The cameraman was standing immediately to the left and behind the gentleman in the foreground. *(W.J. Bladder)*

W.H. Connolly in the racing Star that achieved many successes in Irish competitions in the mid-1920s. (*Michael C. Wylie*)

Bob Wylie with a racing Star at Magilligan Sands. (*Michael C. Wylie*)

A splendid shot of the Star at Magilligan Sands when driven by W.H. Connolly. One can almost smell the sea! (*Michael C. Wylie*)

Hillclimbing at Craigantlet, this time with the same car and driver. (*Michael C. Wylie*)

This GP Alfa-Romeo is pictured outside Fishguard on returning from the Cork GP, mid-1930s. Farewell to Ireland. *(C. Cottrell)*